ANIMALS ARE AMAZING
CROCODILES

BY VALERIE BODDEN

W
FRANKLIN WATTS
LONDON • SYDNEY

This edition published in the UK in 2014 by
Franklin Watts
338 Euston Road
London NW1 3BH

Franklin Watts Australia
Level 17/207 Kent Street
Sydney NSW 2000

First published by Creative Education,
an imprint of the Creative Company.
Copyright © 2010 and 2012 Creative Education

ISBN: 978 1 4451 2955 6
Dewey number: 597.9'82

A CIP catalogue record for this book
is available from the British Library.

Printed in China

Franklin Watts is a division of
Hachette Children's Books
an Hachette UK company
www.hachette.co.uk

Book and cover design by The Design Lab
Art direction by Rita Marshall

Photographs by Alamy (Arco Images GmbH, Jan
Csernoch), Getty Images (Shaen Adey, Annie Griffiths
Belt, James Hager, Jeffrey L. Rotman, Art Wolfe),
iStockphoto (Paul Clarke, George Clerk, Jurie Maree,
Thorsten Rust), Minden Pictures (Suzi Eszterhas,
Mike Parry)

CONTENTS

What are crocodiles?

Crocodiles are big, long **reptiles** with a pointed **snout** and a long tail. They live in or near water. There are 14 different kinds of crocodile in the world.

Crocodiles spend a lot of their time in water.

reptiles animals that have scales and a body that is always as warm or as cold as the air around it.
snout an animal's nose and mouth.

Crocodile skin

A crocodile's back is rough but the scales on its stomach are smooth.

Crocodiles are covered with tough scales to protect their skin. The scales on a crocodile's back are very hard and strong – just like **armour**. Their bodies can be tan, brown, black or green.

armour a strong and tough shell or cover that protects something from being hurt or damaged.

Big crocodiles

Crocodiles are very big animals. They can weigh almost as much as three grown-up people. The largest species of crocodile is the saltwater crocodile. It can grow to be more than six metres long and can weigh more than 1000 kilogrammes!

A crocodile's tail makes up about half of its body length.

Where crocodiles live

Crocodiles live in many places around the world. They prefer to live in hot countries like Australia and on the **continents** of Africa, Asia and North and South America. Crocodiles live along the shores of rivers and lakes. They live in **wetlands**, too. Saltwater crocodiles live by the sea.

continents Earth's seven big pieces of land.
wetlands areas of land that are covered with water. Lots of plants and trees grow in these areas.

Crocodile food

The crocodile on the right has caught a wildebeest. Crocodiles don't chew their food. They tear off big chunks and then swallow them whole.

Crocodiles eat meat.
They eat small animals like birds and fish. They also eat big animals such as deer, wildebeest and zebras! They have very strong jaws and teeth. Crocodiles sometimes drag their **prey** underwater and drown it with a **death roll**.

prey animals that are eaten by other animals.
death roll when crocodiles spin around and around in the water while holding onto their prey with their teeth.

New crocodiles

*A mother crocodile can lay
more than 50 eggs at a time.*

A mother crocodile lays her eggs in a hole dug in sand or in a nest. Baby crocodiles **hatch** from the eggs. Some mother crocodiles will also carry their babies to the water for their first swim. Most baby crocodiles are eaten by other animals and birds. Few will **survive** long enough to grow into an adult crocodile. Crocodiles can live for more than 50 years in the wild.

hatch to break out of an egg.
survive to stay alive when there is great danger.

Lazy crocodiles

Crocodiles spend some of their time out of the water just lying around. If they are too hot, they lie in the shade. If they are cold, they move to a spot in the sun. This is called basking.

Even when crocodiles are out of the water, they still like to be close to it.

Swimming crocodiles

*Some crocodiles can hold their
breath underwater for several hours.*

Crocodiles spend most of their time in water. They are powerful swimmers. They can swim with just their eyes and **nostrils** above the surface of the water, or they can swim with their whole body under the water. Crocodiles wave their strong tails back and forth to push themselves forwards through the water.

nostrils the two holes in a nose.

Crocodiles and people

Today, people around the world go to zoos to see crocodiles. Some people watch crocodiles in the wild. It is exciting to see these big, fierce reptiles anywhere!

Crocodiles in zoos and in the wild like to live with other crocodiles.

A crocodile story

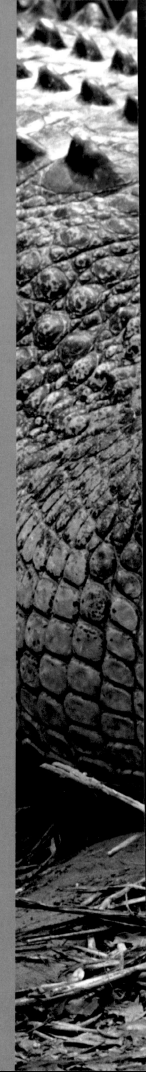

Why do crocodiles have rough skin? People on the continent of Africa tell a story about this. They said that the crocodile once had smooth skin because he stayed in the water all day and came out only at night. The other animals all told the crocodile how much they liked his skin. The crocodile decided to come out during the day to show off his skin. But after a few days the Sun made the crocodile's skin rough and bumpy, and it stayed that way!

Useful information

Read More

Amazing Animals: Alligators and Crocodiles by Sally Morgan
(Franklin Watts, 2013)

Animal Attack: Killer Crocodiles by Alex Woolf (Franklin Watts, 2014)

Saving Wildlife: Wetland Animals by Sonya Newland
(Franklin Watts, 2011)

Websites

http://kids.nationalgeographic.com/kids/animals/creaturefeature/nile-crocodile/
This site has lots of facts about crocodiles, photos and a video of a
mother crocodile helping her babies take their first swim.

http://www.activityvillage.co.uk
Type 'crocodile' into the search box to find lots of crocodile and
alligator activities.

Every effort has been made by the Publishers to ensure that these websites are suitable
for children, that they are of the highest educational value and that they contain no
inappropriate or offensive material. However, because of the nature of the Internet, it
is impossible to guarantee that the contents of these sites will not be altered. We strongly
advise that Internet access is supervised by a responsible adult.

Index